21st Century
Junior Library

INFOGRAPHICS:
SUPPLY CHAINS

Christina Hill

Econo-Graphics Jr.

Published in the United States of America by

Cherry Lake Publishing Group

Ann Arbor, Michigan
www.cherrylakepublishing.com

Reading Adviser: Beth Walker Gambro, MS, Ed., Reading Consultant, Yorkville, IL

Photo Credits: ©Cover, Page 1: ©TarikVision/Getty Images; Page 5: ©elenab/Shutterstock; Page 10: ©Apple, Inc./Wikimedia; Page 8: ©Mohamed Hassan/Pixabay,©OpenClipart-Vectors/Pixabay; Page 9: ©Clker-Free-Vector-Images/Pixabay, ©OpenClipart-Vectors/Pixabay; Page 13: ©Amanita Silvicora/Shutterstock, ©FlowerOFdestiny/Pixabay, ©Revolutionizzed/Shutterstock; Page 17: ©Mind Pixell/Shutterstock, ©valikalina/Shutterstock; Page 18: ©inspiredbythemuse/Pixabay, ©OpenClipart-Vectors/Pixabay, ©valikalina/Shutterstock; Page 19: ©AlexZel/ Pixabay, ©carina/Shutterstock, ©DavidRockDesign/Pixabay, ©Mix3r/Shutterstock, ©OpenClipart-Vectors/Pixabay, ©Satheesh Sankaran/ Pixabay; Page 20: ©Mix3r/Shutterstock; Page 21: ©Clker-Free-Vector Images/Pixabay, ©Wise ant/Shutterstock; Page 22: ©Clker-Free-Vector- Images/Pixabay, ©George Mutambuka/Pixabay, ©iKandy/Shutterstock, ©monique_hernandez/Pixabay, ©OpenClipart-Vectors/Pixabay, ©Satheesh Sankaran/Pixabay, ©Werner Moser/Pixabay

Cherry Lake Press is an imprint of Cherry Lake Publishing Group.

Library of Congress Cataloging-in-Publication Data
Names: Hill, Christina, author.
Title: Infographics. Supply chains / Christina Hill.
Other titles: Supply chains
Description: Ann Arbor, Michigan : Cherry Lake Publishing, [2023] | Series: Econo-graphics Jr. | Includes bibliographical references and index. | Audience: Grades 2-3 | Summary: "How do supply chains work? In the Econo-Graphics Jr. series, young readers will examine economy-related issues from many angles, all portrayed through visual elements. Income, budgeting, investing, supply and demand, global markets, inflation, and more are covered. Each book highlights pandemic-era impacts as well. Created with developing readers in mind, charts, graphs, maps, and infographics provide key content in an engaging and accessible way. Books include an activity, glossary, index, suggested reading and websites, and a bibliography"— Provided by publisher.
Identifiers: LCCN 2022037923 | ISBN 9781668919217 (hardcover) | ISBN 9781668920237 (paperback) | ISBN 9781668922897 (pdf) | ISBN 9781668921562 (ebook)
Subjects: LCSH: Business logistics—Juvenile literature.
Classification: LCC HD38.5 .H5527 2023 | DDC 658.5—dc23/eng/20220818
LC record available at https://lccn.loc.gov/2022037923
Cherry Lake Publishing Group would like to acknowledge the work of the Partnership for 21st Century Learning, a network of Battelle for Kids. Please visit http://www.battelleforkids.org/networks/p21 for more information.

Printed in the United States of America
Corporate Graphics

Before embracing a career as an author, **Christina Hill** received a bachelor's degree in English from the University of California, Irvine, and a graduate degree in literature from California State University, Long Beach. When she is not writing about various subjects from sports to economics, Christina can be found hiking, mastering yoga handstands, or curled up with a classic novel. Christina lives in sunny Southern California with her husband, two sons, and beloved dog, Pepper Riley.

CONTENTS

WHAT IS A SUPPLY CHAIN?

A **supply chain** is a system chain. The links in the chain include people. They could be workers or business owners. They include equipment. They could be tools or delivery trucks. They include technology. They could be robots or computer programs for designing goods.

These links in the chain work together to make goods. They work together to **distribute** goods.

Key Supply Chain Links

Supplier This is the start of the chain. It includes the raw materials used to make the goods.

Producer This is the factory where the goods are made.

Retailer This is the store that sells the goods to customers.

Customer The customer buys the goods. Then the chain starts all over again.

TYPES OF SUPPLY CHAINS

Some supply chains are simple. They move in a straight line. Goods move directly from supplier to producer to **consumer**.

The goal of a good supply chain is to meet **demand**. Customers should get what they want. They should get it quickly and at the right price.

Balancing Service, Cash, and Cost for Success

Service

Get the right items to the right customers. Get them to customers at the right time and the right cost. This improves customer satisfaction.

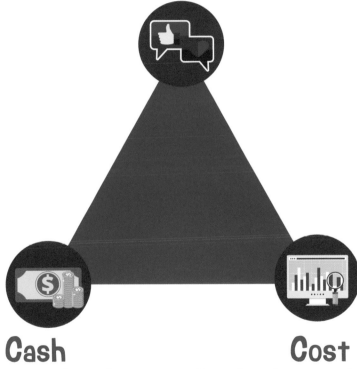

Cash

Companies must keep large amounts of raw materials. They must keep finished goods on hand. If needed, they can quickly turn them into cash.

Cost

Keeping the cost of production down is important. Producers can buy more supplies at a lower cost.

The Efficiency of McDonald's Supply Chain

Materials

McDonald's grows its own lettuce, tomatoes, and potatoes. It raises its own cattle.

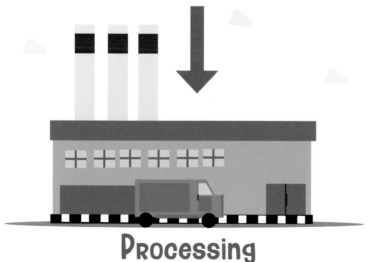

Processing

All food products are processed in McDonald's factories. They must meet the company's standards.

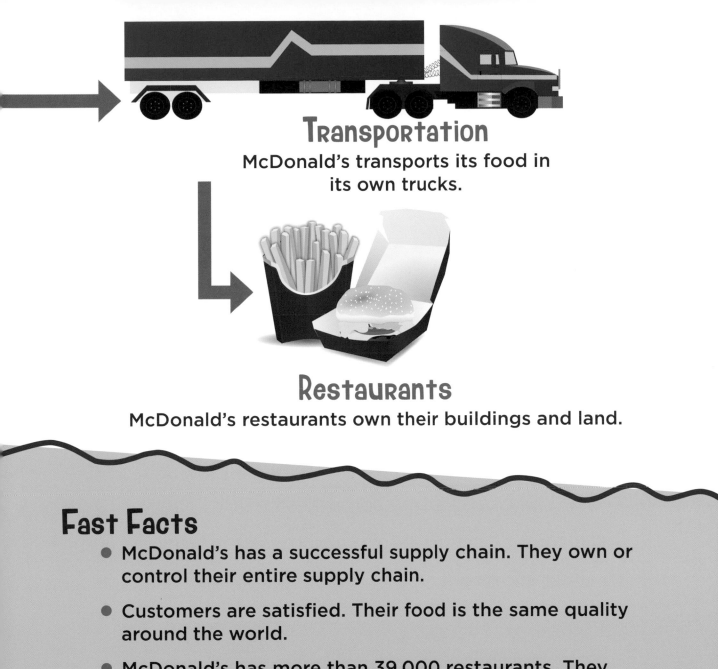

Transportation

McDonald's transports its food in its own trucks.

Restaurants

McDonald's restaurants own their buildings and land.

Fast Facts

- McDonald's has a successful supply chain. They own or control their entire supply chain.

- Customers are satisfied. Their food is the same quality around the world.

- McDonald's has more than 39,000 restaurants. They serve more than 69 million customers every day.

SUPPLY CHAIN MANAGEMENT

Goods and services should move quickly through the supply chain. A supply chain manager makes sure this happens.

Supply chain managers watch the supply chain. They make sure each link is healthy. Their job is to cut costs and fix problems. They work to avoid **shortages**.

Five Parts of Supply Chain Management

Plan
What materials are needed? Will they be local or from another country?

Source
Which supplier is right for product materials and offers the best price?

Make
Who can create and put together the materials? Who can package the materials into goods?

Deliver
How should the finished goods be delivered?

Return
What will the return policy be? How can customers return unwanted or broken items?

Transport Factors to Consider

Cost
A $1,000 air shipment will cost only $200 by sea.

Travel Time
Airplanes are the fastest choice for long distances. Ships can take several weeks to reach the same location.

Location
Is it local or global?

Limitations
Do the goods need to be kept cold? Are the goods too large to fit in a truck?

Availability
What if the weather slows road travel or cancels flights?

Planet Health
Airplanes create 44 times more carbon dioxide than ships do. They are a less Earth-friendly choice.

Fair Trade and Supply Chains

Fair trade is a global group. It is made up of producers, businesses, and customers. They push for human rights and fair **wages**. They push for Earth-friendly practices in their supply chains.

Fair trade coffee sells five times faster than other coffee.

In 2018, fair trade products earned $11.4 billion in worldwide sales.

More than 80% of fair trade cotton comes from India.

Global Supply Chain of a Smartphone

1 Design

The United States provides the software for the microchip design.

3 Materials

Silicon is mined in the United States. It is processed in Japan and South Korea.

2021, Boston Consulting Group

② Equipment
The equipment is made in the United States, Japan, and Europe.

④ Manufacturing
Microchips are made in Taiwan and Malaysia. Then they are put into smartphones in China.

SUPPLY CHAIN DISRUPTIONS

Many things can **disrupt** a supply chain. They can cause the links in the chain to break. Throughout history, natural disasters have caused many supply chain disruptions.

In 2020, the COVID-19 pandemic started. It destroyed supply chains across the world.

Supply Chains of the Future

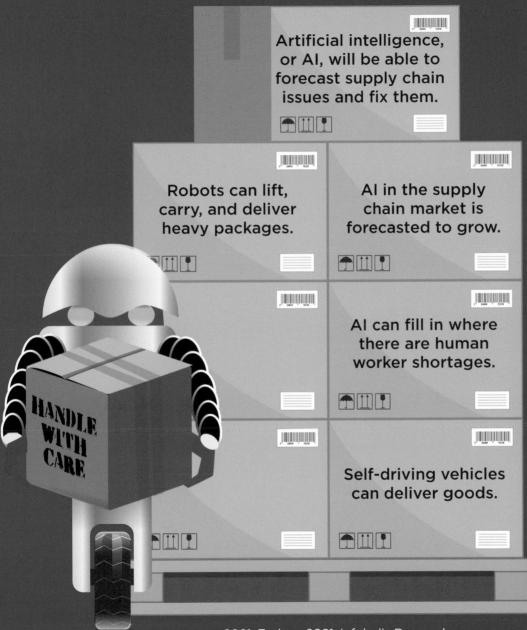

Artificial intelligence, or AI, will be able to forecast supply chain issues and fix them.

Robots can lift, carry, and deliver heavy packages.

AI in the supply chain market is forecasted to grow.

AI can fill in where there are human worker shortages.

Self-driving vehicles can deliver goods.

HANDLE WITH CARE

2021, Forbes; 2021, Infoholic Research

When the Supply Chain Breaks

Hurricane Katrina wipes out power lines and transportation routes. This disrupts many supply chains. Most companies wait for the port of New Orleans to be restored. Why? One ship carries as much as 15 railcars can. One ship carries as much as 60 semi-trucks.

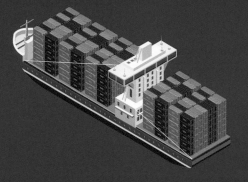

2005

2007

Boeing is an airplane company. They make 787 Dreamliner planes. The supplier of bolts for these planes fails. Boeing buys bolts from local hardware stores. This temporarily fixes the supply chain.

When the Supply Chain Breaks

An earthquake and tsunami in Japan close a factory. It is the only factory that makes a special paint. U.S. car companies Ford and Chrysler use this paint. The companies delay production. They offer cars in colors that don't need this paint.

2011

2014

The Disney movie *Frozen* makes $1.2 billion. But Disney did not plan for the huge success. People want toys based on the movie. Toy shelves are emptied instantly. The company scrambles to make more. Fans are disappointed in the long wait.

The 2020 Supply Chain Fail of Toilet Paper

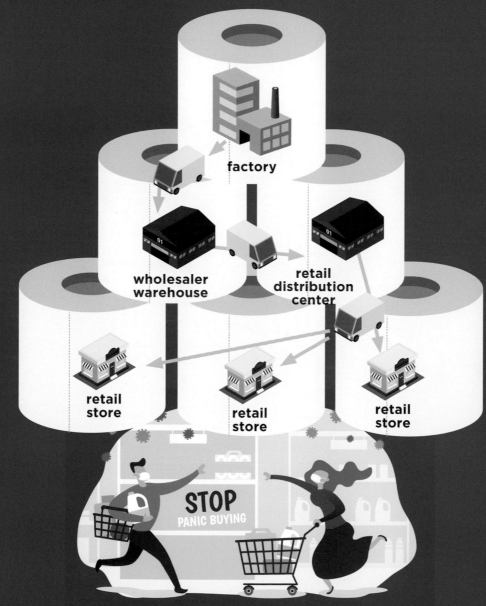

The 2020 Supply Chain Fail of Toilet Paper

During the COVID-19 pandemic, stores had no toilet paper. People had rushed to buy it all!

Toilet paper runs on a simple supply chain. What happened?

Consumer demand was too high. There was no way the supply chain could meet it.

On March 12, 2020, toilet paper sales went up. They rose 734% higher than in 2019.

By March 23, 2020, 70% of U.S. stores had no toilet paper left. This included online sites.

2020, Forbes

ACTIVITY
Become a Supply Chain Manager

Your mom says you can use the kitchen to make cereal bar treats. They are for your school bake sale. Use the supply chain below to help you manage the job.

Raw Materials
butter, cereal, marshmallows

Supplier
grocery store

Transportation
family car

Production
you in your family's kitchen

Transportation
your bike

Retail
the school bake sale

Customers
students and families

1. Could your supply chain change? What if the store didn't have cereal? What if your bike got a flat tire going to school?

2. Look over this supply chain. What do you think is the most important link? Explain your answer.